Magical Experiments with Light & Color

Text: Paula Navarro & Àngels Jiménez
Illustrations: Bernadette Cuxart

W9-BLH-622

BARRON'S

Contents

Waves of light, 4

What color do you see?, 6

I've got a hole in my hand!, 8

Let's make use of the sun, 10

Hidden colors, 12

The eyes have memory!, 14

Wavy squares, 16

The rainbow disc, 18

Colored bubble, 20

Aim at the balloon!, 22

The elastic straw, 24

Magical light, 26

Oil painting, 28

Disobedient drawings, 30

Milky sunset, 32

A movie theater in your hands, 34

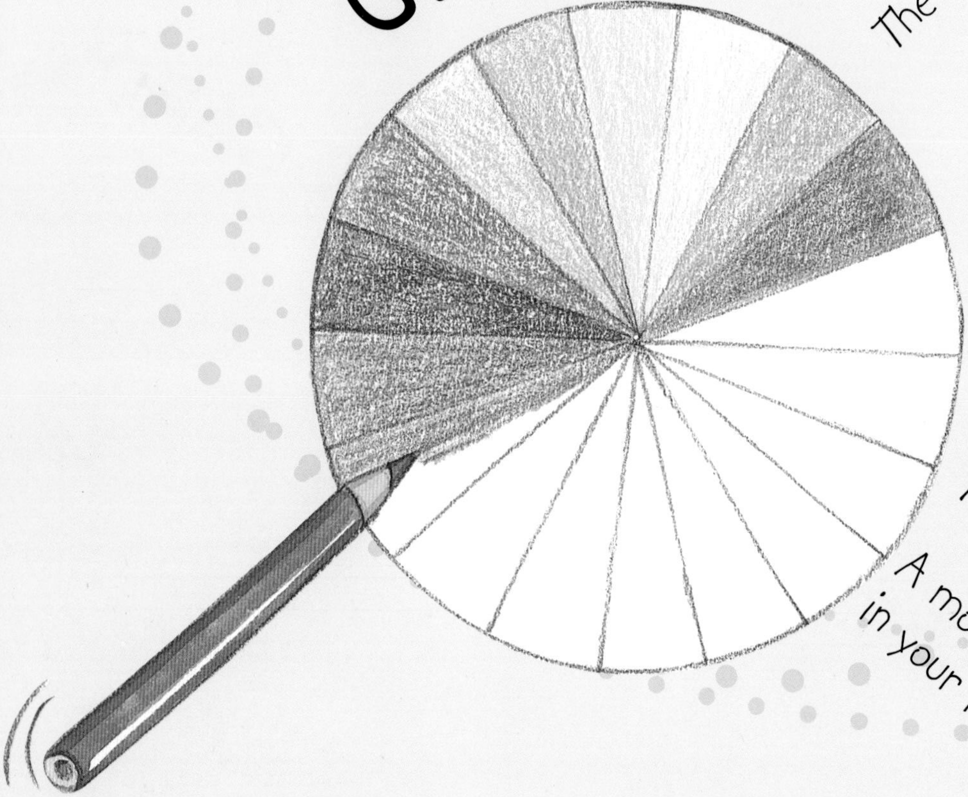

Objectives of this book

We present you with the second book in the series of four "Magic science" volumes. In this case, *Magical Experiments with Light and Color* is aimed at boys and girls in the age range of 6 to 12 years old, to explain a topic that is complex and at the same time fascinating: the creation and behavior of light and color.

In this second book on science and practical tasks, the boys and girls tackle a topic whose understanding is more abstract than the first (sound), as the idea is that they resolve the enigmas of scientific knowledge gradually and in a fun way.

The 16 experiments that are found in this book explain what light is and what it consists of, the path that light follows to reach our eyes; how our eyes and our brains compose images; what the phenomena of light interference, refraction, and scattering are; what an optical illusion is and how it is generated; how colors are created; and how sunlight affects our lives.

Magical Experiments with Light and Color is a compendium of highly visual and magical experiments on a topic that is very familiar but difficult to explain and that, with the help of the practical tasks, will become easy to understand!

Waves of light

You will need:
- Wide elastic
- Paints or felt-tipped pens for decorating
- Glue
- Pencil
- Ruler
- Wooden sticks (at least 36)
- Scissors

1 Paint the wooden sticks in different colors. You can use felt-tipped pens or watercolors. But paint them on the front *and* on the back! Try to make the colors varied so that the end effect will look cooler.

2 Take the elastic and measure a length at least twice as long as your outstretched arms and cut it.

3 Leave 6 cm from one end of the elastic, which will be the margin serving to hang it when you have finished it all. And from this point, make marks on the elastic every 6 cm, where you will place the wooden sticks. It's best to use a ruler designed for the purpose!

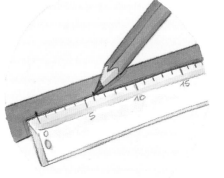

4 Apply a little glue in the center of the wooden stick and glue it to the elastic. So that it is well centered, a good trick is to measure it with the ruler and mark the point with a pencil.

5 Glue all the wooden sticks onto the elastic, on the marks, alternating the colors. Don't use too much glue, otherwise it will go over the edges and be difficult to clean.

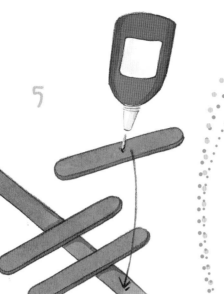

Why does it happen?

You have just made a transversal wave! And what's that? When you tap the first wooden stick, you create a vertical movement (downward) that is transmitted along the elastic and to all the little sticks, and this makes us see a moving wave. The light from the sun, lightbulb, or fluorescent light **always travels through a wave** like the one you made. But you cannot see it. The sun's energy that warms us and gives us light arrives in waves of light!

6 Try it out!

Call a friend and ask him to hold one end of the elastic while you hold the other. When the elastic is stretched… tap one of the sticks suddenly. ARE YOU READY? NOW! Do you see how the wave is transmitted and bounces?

What color do you see?

1 Draw around the plate on the cardboard and cut along the line. Do the same to the white construction paper.

You will need:
- White construction paper
- A piece of cardboard
- A dessert plate
- Thick string
- Scissors
- Stick of glue
- Black felt-tipped pen
- A wooden stick
- Ruler

2 Now you make some folds. Fold the construction paper in half and then fold it in half again. The four sections of the circle must be well marked. And then fold it in half once more!

3 Unfold the construction paper and go over the fold marks with the pen, but only mark the lines that divide the circle on one of the halves.

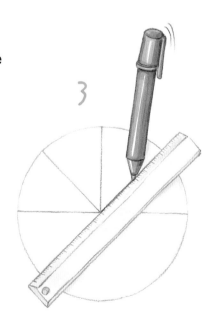

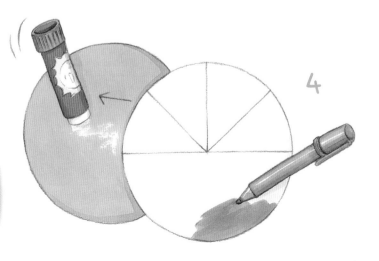

4 Carefully glue the construction paper onto the cardboard. Paint the half of the circle without the fold marks in black (you could also use a piece of black construction paper).

5 Now mark three 6 mm arcs in each consecutive sector separated by 1 mm (ask an adult to help you for this step). If you haven't got a compass, you can make one at home: Use the stick, the string, and the pencil (as shown in the drawing).

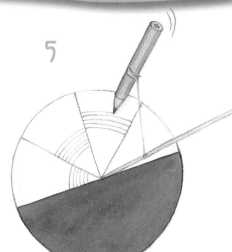

Why does it happen?

When you spin the disc fast, you can manage to see the colors red and blue. How is this possible, if the disc is only painted black? Well, because **white is the sum of all the colors,** and to see the color red your eyes use a very delicate part, called cones. As some cones are faster than others, it's as if the eye didn't have time to add all the colors together for you to see the color white. So the eye does so gradually and you only see the colors red and blue.

6 Try it out!

Go over the arcs you have drawn with the pen. When you have drawn them all, place the stick in the middle of the circle and make it spin very fast... You can try and use it for hypnotizing, but first say what you see in the circle!

I've got a hole in my hand!

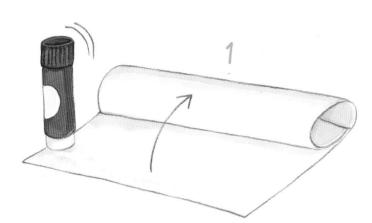

1 Take the sheet of paper and roll it into a tube, but be careful not to flatten it! Don't press strongly, just hold it. Stick it with the glue.

You will need:
- Tape
- Stick of glue
- A sheet of 8½" x 11" white paper
- (A hand)

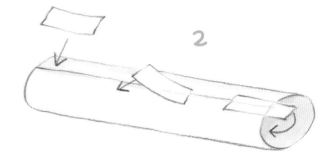

2 Strengthen it with the tape. It's best to fix it at three points, at the top, at the bottom, and in the middle, so that it is well secured!

3 Place the tube in front of your eye—yes, as if you were a pirate looking for a treasure island!

4 Cover the other eye with your empty hand, placing it so that it touches the side of the tube. Don't get your hand or your eye mixed up!

5

Why does it happen?

Your eyes work like two cameras. They receive the light that reaches them and take two photos that are similar but not identical, as each eye is in a different position. Your brain combines the images from both eyes to form a single image. This process is called **image composition**. If the images are found very close to your eyes, your brain places one image on top of the other, and that's why it looks like your hand has a hole in it!

5 Move the hand over your eye away slightly, but not the hand that is holding the tube, otherwise you'll drop it! Do so carefully, because the hand you separate from your eye must continue touching the side of the tube.

6

6 Try it out!
Move your hand in front of your eye forward and backward and you will notice that… Oh! What has happened to your hand? It's got a hole in it!

Let's make use of the sun

You will need:
- A metal box (could be a food tin)
- Black construction paper
- Aluminum foil
- Scissors
- Tape
- A piece of glass
- A fresh egg
- A mirror

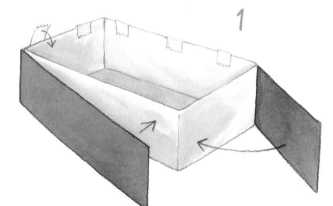

1 Find a metal box or tin that is quite large, such as a large asparagus tin. Line the outside with black construction paper and secure it well with tape.

2 Line the inside of the box with aluminum foil. If necessary, also secure it with tape.

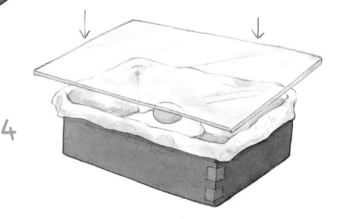

3 Carefully break an egg in the box, on the aluminum foil. Be careful! Try to break it well so that no pieces of eggshell fall in!

4 Place the glass on the box to form a transparent lid that will enable you to see the egg, but will leave the box well sealed so that the inside can warm up.

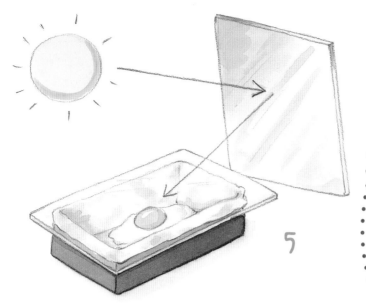

5 Take the mirror and, holding it firmly in your hand, place it in front of a window. Hold it slightly tilted so that the sunlight is reflected from the mirror into the box where the egg is. It's better if you conduct this experiment outside!

Why does it happen?

As well as illuminating us, sunlight warms us. If you can direct a large amount of heat to the same place, you can do many things, such as heat a greenhouse the whole winter even though it is cold outside. In this experiment, **you have taken advantage of the sunlight** and you have imitated the greenhouse effect by lining the box with aluminum foil, as this helps the sun's rays have a better distribution and warm faster. The heat you obtained was enough to cook the egg, as if it had been in an oven.

6 Try it out!
You need to be patient and not alter the position at all, even if you are sweating! Well, if you really must, you can move... but take into account that it will be like turning off the oven suddenly with the food remaining half-cooked! Wait for the egg to cook! Yes, yes, just with the help of the heat from the sun! Well, you could add a little oil if you like!

Hidden colors

1 Mark a rectangle on the filter paper with the pencil. You will need a ruler for this, of course! Draw it on the widest and longest part of the paper to obtain a longer and better defined strip.

You will need:
- Alcohol
- A glass
- A spoon
- Pencil
- A black pen
- Porous paper (such as a coffee filter or newspaper)
- Ruler

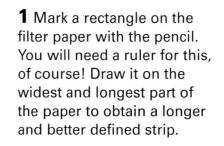

2 Cut the paper following the pencil mark. Be careful not to go over the line!

3 Hang the strip of paper over the spoon. Place the spoon on the glass horizontally and face down, so that the paper strip falls vertically inside the glass. The length of the strip of paper must coincide with the depth of the glass, but without touching the bottom of it. It will look like a banner!

4 Take the spoon out for a moment and pour a little alcohol into the glass, about two fingers' width high. Alcohol for disinfecting cuts will do perfectly!

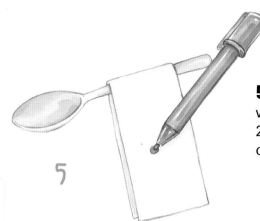

5 Mark a black dot with the pen about 2 cm from the end of the paper strip.

6 Try it out!

Place the spoon back on the glass as before. The end of the strip must be wetted in the alcohol so that it absorbs it—as if it were drinking it!

If you are patient, you will see that as the alcohol rises up the paper strip, it drags the black dot you have marked upward and leaves a band of colors that were not there before! Wow! Where did they come from?

Why does it happen?

Did you think that the ink in pens and felt-tipped markers is a single color? Well, you have just demonstrated that, in fact, the ink from which they are made is often a mixture of colors, or **pigments**! You have seen it by conducting **chromatography** with the pen ink. The same thing is done in laboratories to separate mixtures and to discover what objects are really comprised of. You need to use thin paper, because then the alcohol can leave the mark of the components.

The eyes have memory!

1 Place the glass upside down on the construction paper and use it as a pattern for drawing a circle. Then cut out the circle.

2 Draw and cut two more circles, the same as the first.

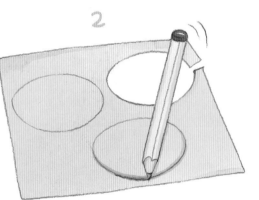

You will need:
- Light-colored construction paper
- Pencil
- A glass
- Stick of glue
- Scissors
- Felt-tipped pens
- Thin elastic or string
- A paper clip

3 Make a drawing you like on the circles, such as a portrait of somebody you know. Make another drawing on the other circle, so that it fits with the other drawing and is related with it (for example, sunglasses). It's important that they are at the correct level when you turn them over. The third circle stays blank. You can go over the drawings or color them in with pens so that they stand out better.

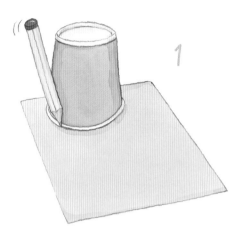

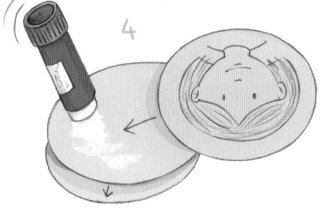

4 Glue the three circles so that the blank one is in the middle. The two with drawings must be on opposite sides, that is, one facing north and the other facing south.

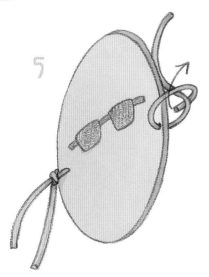

5 Mark a point at each side of the circle and make a hole using the paper clip. If you can't make a hole, try using a ballpoint pen. Then thread some elastic or string through the holes and tie them together well with knots.

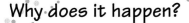

6 Try it out!

When it's ready, the great moment has arrived: Turn the elastic with your fingers! Then you will see both drawings superimposed: the person wearing sunglasses! Yes!

Why does it happen?

When you see an image, the light that reaches the objects around you bounces off them and reaches your eyes. From there, the light travels a long path until **the image is formed in part of the eye called the retina** and then it reaches the brain, where it is interpreted. This process is quite slow, and when you see two images very close together, the brain retains the first one as it starts seeing the second. That's why you see the sunglasses on the woman's face, despite the fact that the images are very different!

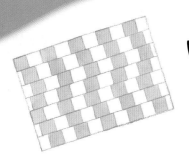

Wavy squares

You will need:

- Ruler
- Felt-tipped pen
- Pencil
- Sheet of white paper

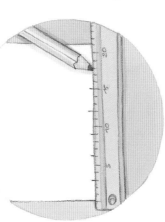

1 Place the sheet of paper horizontally. Use the pencil and ruler to make the dots between lines separated 3 cm apart to draw them afterward. You should mark both sides of the paper; then you will obtain very straight lines!

2 Draw the lines by joining the dots together. You will end up with 6 lines, that is, 7 rows.

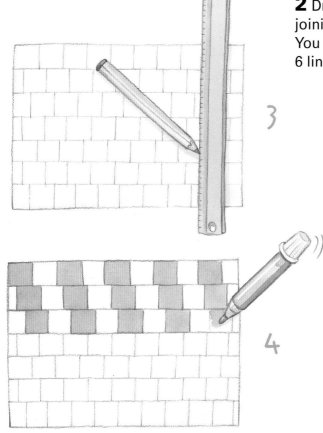

3 Now fill the sheet of paper with squares, following these instructions: If you start marking them at the margin in the first row, start a bit further along in the second row compared to the first (approximately 1 cm). In the third row, displace them by 2 cm, with respect to the first row… but in the fourth row, mark them as in the second, the fifth like in the first, the sixth like the second, and the seventh like in the third. It's not difficult!

4 Go over the squares you have just drawn with the pen. Be careful with the order, otherwise it will be a mess! Don't get confused; you should paint them alternately, OK?

Why does it happen?

When your eyes see, they reconstruct the image in the brain, which fills in the missing information. The brain gathers a lot of information and draws conclusions regarding what things are like. But sometimes the brain tricks you!

Then an **optical illusion** occurs, like in the experiment you have just conducted. The same thing happens when you look at the moon and it appears so close. Your brain compares the moon with other objects that are closer (buildings and trees, etc.) and also interprets the moon as being close.

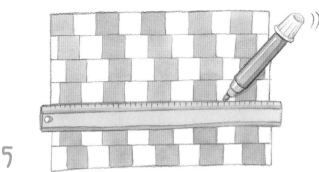

5

5 To obtain the final effect, go over the horizontal lines with the pen. You should use the ruler to obtain straight lines.

6

6 Try it out!
Place the sheet of paper some distance from your eyes and observe the whole set of squares and lines. Are you sure you drew straight lines?

The rainbow disc

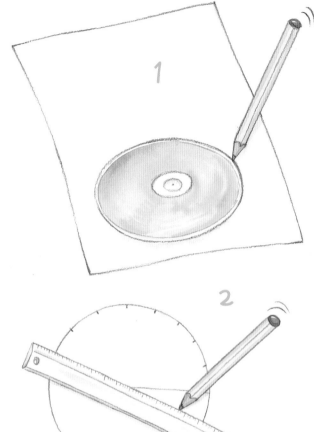

1 Draw around the CD on the sheet of paper with the pencil. Mark also the center point. Remember that it should be an old CD you don't play anymore, because you won't be able to get it back… No, no! The Beatles are your parents' favorite!

2 Use the ruler to divide the circle in half. Using this line as the reference, mark a point about every 2 cm around the circle. Then draw the lines joining the dots with the center. You can draw this line to the center of the circle (its radius) or draw from the top to bottom of the circle (its diameter).

You will need:
- An old CD
- Stick of glue
- Sheet of white paper
- Pencil
- Colored pencils (the 7 colors of the rainbow)
- Ruler
- A marble

3 Color in the resulting sectors: They will end up like pie pieces! Be careful to follow the order of the colors of the rainbow: red, orange, yellow, green, blue, indigo, and violet. Very eye-catching!

4 Cut out the circle following the outline drawn with the pencil, but without cutting any of the pieces! Keep your hands from shaking!

5 Glue the circle on the CD with the stick of glue (on the white part, of course). Make a hole in the paper, corresponding with the hole in the middle of the CD, and fit the marble there.

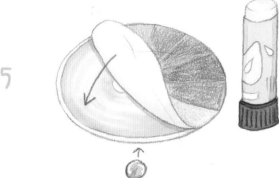

Why does it happen?

When you spin the circle very fast, all the colors are combined and form the white color that you see. You have just demonstrated that **white light is the sum of all the colors of the rainbow (red, orange, yellow, green, blue, indigo, and violet), whereas black is the opposite: It is the absence of color.** That's why you see the color of each object, because when an object receives white light (the sum of all the colors), it absorbs all the colors apart from its own color, which means that you see the color of each object.

6 Try it out!

Place it on a table and… make your colored circle spin as fast as possible! Faster, faster! What colors did you see? All of them? Or none? Whoops!

Colored bubble

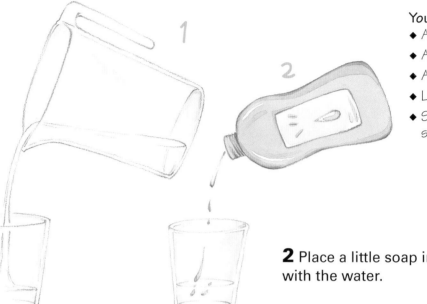

1 Fill the two containers with water: the jug and the bowl. How generous! But you don't need more than two fingers' width of water; you don't need to waste it, do you?

You will need:
- ◆ A jug of water
- ◆ A low tray or bowl
- ◆ A glass
- ◆ Liquid soap
- ◆ Several drinking straws

2 Place a little soap in the glass with the water.

3 Wet the straw in the soapy water. You should obtain a soapy bubble mixture—like a mini bubble bath! Cool!

4 Take the straw that you have just wet in the soap, fill your lungs with air, and blow a bubble on the water in the bowl. Yes, very large!

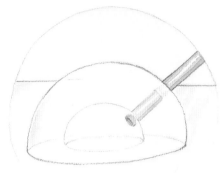

5 Try doing the same on a table (its better if it has a glass surface) and blow one bubble inside the other! Even more difficult!

5

6 Try it out!

Place a dark background behind the bubble, such as black construction paper, and you will see a colorful bubble and how it changes color as you move it from one side to the other! Also, if you blow gently onto a soap bubble, you will see that the colors of the bubble create little waves. How amazing!

6

Why does it happen?

What you saw in the bubble, as well as being a lovely sight, is the **phenomenon of interference** that occurs when several waves of light coincide at the same place and are positioned one over the other. You have seen that light is a wave. Well, in this experiment, what you see is that many waves of light coincide on the surface of the bubble and are reflected in your eyes. That's why you see bands of colors!

Aim at the balloon!

You will need:
- A magnifying glass
- Different colored balloons
- A black balloon
- A white balloon
- Black felt-tipped pen

1 Blow up one of the balloons. Any one— well, NOT the WHITE one OR the BLACK one.

2 On a sunny day, focus a magnifying glass in the sun so that the light falls on the balloon. Wait for the balloon to burst. BOOM! Don't be naughty! Don't scare anybody! If the balloon doesn't burst, make it burst yourself, with your hand or an instrument to help you (the tip of a pen, for example).

3 Blow up another balloon, but not the WHITE or the BLACK one. This time, mark it with the pen.

4 Focus the sunlight on the balloon again and see whether focusing the magnifying glass on the black spot will burst this balloon sooner or later than the previous one. BOOM! Be careful with your eyes!

5 Now blow up the BLACK balloon and repeat the same procedure as for the previous two balloons. See whether it bursts sooner or later than the rest…

Why does it happen?

With the magnifying glass, you **concentrate the sun's rays onto a single point.** When it receives enough heat, the point is capable of burning the balloon rubber and making it burst… But always in the same way? You have seen that the black balloon or the black spot on the other balloon burst sooner. Why? Because black absorbs all the light and makes the balloon heat up easier. And why doesn't the white balloon burst? Well, because white reflects the light, such that the balloon does not warm up.

6 Try it out!
Finally, blow up the WHITE balloon! Yes, AT LAST! Also focus the sunlight on it with the magnifying glass. Now what happens? Does it burst or not?

23

The elastic straw

You will need:
- Oil
- A jug of water
- A tall glass
- A straw

1 Fill the glass about halfway with water... well, no, a little higher than halfway. Super duper!

2 Place the straw in the glass and look at it from one side. Don't choose a transparent straw, because it might have a camouflage effect that prevents you from seeing what happens to the straw.

3 Move the straw slowly in the glass and you will notice that it splits into two parts. It really looks like two different straws! Oooh!

4 Add a little oil, about a couple of fingers' width on top of the water. The oil doesn't mix with the water because of the different densities of the liquids... we'll study that later, don't worry!

24

Why does it happen?

The light that enters the glass is diverted when it leaves the water and it looks like the straw is broken into pieces! This phenomenon is light diversion, which is called **refraction**. When you add the oil, the light is diverted again, so that it looks like the straw is broken into three pieces, despite the fact that nothing has happened to it.

The same thing happens when you go to the beach and you want to catch a fish under the water. It appears closer than it really is and that's why it's so difficult to catch!

5 . Place the straw back in the water and oil. Do you notice the division? You haven't got blurred vision, no, no... Move the straw to see what happens. You have a triple division! Ooooooh!

6 Try it out!
Compare the optical effect of how you see the straw when you place it in the water and in the water and the oil. Is the straw alive or what?

Magical light

1 Cut a small piece of cellophane that enables you to completely cover the flashlight lens. Do so for the three colors you have.

2 Cover the part of the flashlight that emits the light with the cellophane and secure it with tape, as if you were wrapping a present!

You will need:
- Tape
- Three flashlights (with batteries!)
- Scissors
- Red, blue, and green cellophane

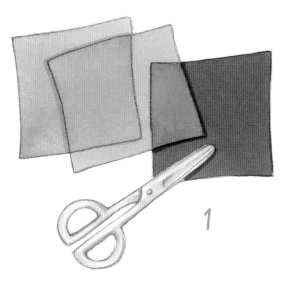

1

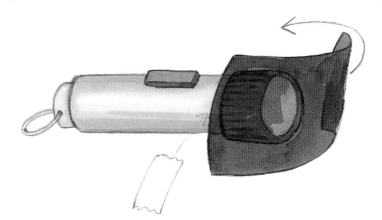

2

3 Now cover the other two flashlights the same way as you did for the first. You should place a different color cellophane on each flashlight. Hey, why do you need three?

4 Very important for the experiment: Turn off the light! Ooh! How scary!

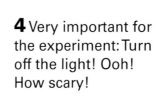

3

4

5

5 Now it's time to test the filters! Do so by focusing the light onto a wall or table, whichever is a nice pure white color. Can you see the three colors well?

Why does it happen?

The colors red, blue, and green were chosen because they are **the primary colors of light**, from which you can obtain the other colors. In fact, computer screens obtain the colors thanks to a combination of very small dots (pixels) that mix these three colors and create others. Inside your eyes, there are light-sensitive cells, called cones and rods: The former enable us to see the primary colors and their combinations and the latter enable us to see the intensity of the light.

6

6 Try it out!
Finally, a delicate step: You have to make the three colors coincide in the center. What happens? Have you created a new color? Wow!

Oil painting

You will need:
- A sheet of blank paper
- Oil
- Colored pencils
- Pencil
- A fine paintbrush
- Black felt-tipped pen (optional)

1 You need to be an artist for this step. Draw a picture with the pencil with three different figures. Make it fun, like the sun with a bird and some trees.

2 Color some of the figures as you like, but not all of them! Spectacular!

3 Place some oil on a plate and some newspaper underneath the paper, ready for painting the rest of the figures with the oil. Remember that cleanliness is one of the most important things in life!

4 Wet the paintbrush in the oil and then paint the figures you have left blank. Be careful not to go over the lines too much, because oil tends to spread!

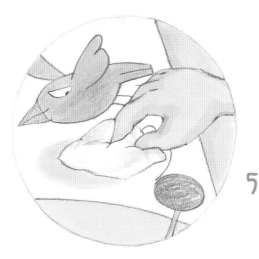

5

Why does it happen?

You must have observed the paper wrapping little sandwiches: **The paper stained with oil is more transparent!** So, if you hold your drawing against the light, the areas painted with oil are brighter, as they are more transparent and allow more light to pass through. If you place the paper so that the light does not reach it directly, the areas painted with oil look darker.

5 Dry the parts you have painted in oil with a little paper so that it absorbs the excess. All very clean!

6

6 Try it out!
Approach the window and move the drawing to see the contrast and you will notice that the parts painted with oil shine or are dark, depending on how the light reaches them. AMAZING, no!?!

Disobedient drawings

You will need:

- ◆ Tape
- ◆ A tall glass
- ◆ A jug of water
- ◆ Wooden sticks
- ◆ Felt-tipped pen
- ◆ A spoon
- ◆ Sugar

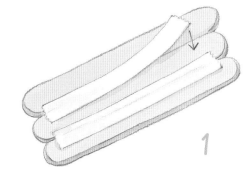

1

1 Take a couple of wooden sticks. If they are very thin, you can place several together side by side and secure them at the back with tape. Do so carefully so that they don't end up at different heights!

2 Draw a really great picture with the pen that occupies the middle of the sticks. We've drawn a house with a chimney, with smoke coming out of it!

3 Make an improvised support for the sticks so that they stand up! You can make it by cutting a stick in half, bending the tip slightly, and securing it with tape at the back! There! Like photograph frames!

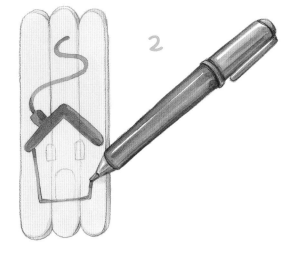

2

3

4

4 Place the sticks behind the glass. Make sure that they are very straight and you can see the drawing. You might need to crouch down slightly to see it well!

5 Take a jug and fill the glass to the top so that the water is higher than the drawing you have made.

Why does it happen?

The little house you drew did not increase its rooms while you were filling up the glass with water, but rather this experiment is another case of **light refraction**, not only because of the water, which scatters the light, but because of the glass. With the glass, you obtain a magnifying glass effect, which means that everything looks larger! Also, the water makes all the drawings turn around!

6 Try it out!

Whoops! What happened? It looks like the little house has grown and now it's a really big house! The chimney has also changed places! Didn't you draw it on the left? Well now it's on the right!
You can also try drawing other simple shapes to see what happens... Wow!

Milky sunset

1 Pour a little water into the wide transparent container. Fill it about 3 fingers' width high; you don't need a ruler.

You will need:
- A wide transparent container
- Water
- Milk
- A flashlight (with batteries)

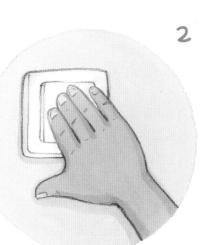

2 The next step is crucial: Turn off the light! In order to be able to see and avoid bumping into furniture, you should have the flashlight in your other hand!

3 Place the flashlight next to the container so that it shines on it. You should see the ray of light go through the water. Wow!

4 Pour a little milk in the container without turning off the flashlight and without turning on the lights! Be careful to avoid spilling the milk.

5

5 Wait for the milk to mix well with the water, as if you were making a sauce in which all the ingredients should be mixed!

Why does it happen?

When you add a little milk to the water, you imitate what happens in the sky with the sunlight: **The white light is dispersed.** That's why, when the sky is blue in the morning, it's as if you were looking at the flashlight's light from the side: You see the shorter wave of light, which is the color blue. In the afternoon, the sun is at the horizon and the light has to travel a greater distance. Then it's as if you were looking at the flashlight's light directly: You see the longest waves of light, which are orange and red.

6 Try it out!

Observe the result from above. Wow! It looks like you have the sunset in the container!
If the light from your flashlight is white, try illuminating the container with a warmer, yellower tone and you will see that the result is very pretty!

6

A movie theater in your hands

You will need:
- Light-colored 8½" x 11" construction paper
- Skewer
- Stick of glue
- Pencil
- Scissors
- Paper clips or small pegs
- Felt-tipped pen (optional)

1 Fold the construction paper in half. Fold it with your hands, but do so carefully so that the ends coincide, OK? Then cut the paper along the marked middle. You will have two pieces, smaller than the first.

2 Be careful! You must now do the same with the two pieces as you did in the first step. That is, fold them in half and cut them.
How many pieces are you left with?

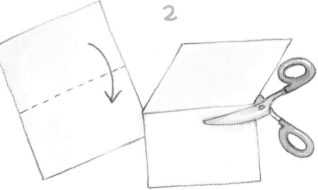

3 Yes, there are 4 pieces! Now think of a drawing in which there is a figure that should move…
We've drawn a teddy bear wearing a hat!

4 Place one piece on top of the other and secure them with paper clips or small pegs. To make the drawing in four steps, press firmly with the pencil so that the main figure leaves an impression on the paper underneath. It is important to press firmly, except on the part of the figure that moves. For example, if you want the teddy bear to take his hat off, trace everything apart from the arm that will make the movement.

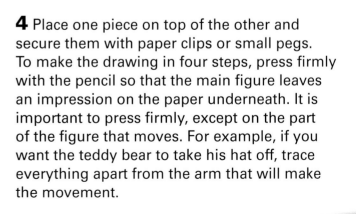

5 Very carefully apply glue to the backs of the paper and stick them together one after the other. The movement scenes must be in order! Glue the skewer in the middle so that it emerges from the top slightly.

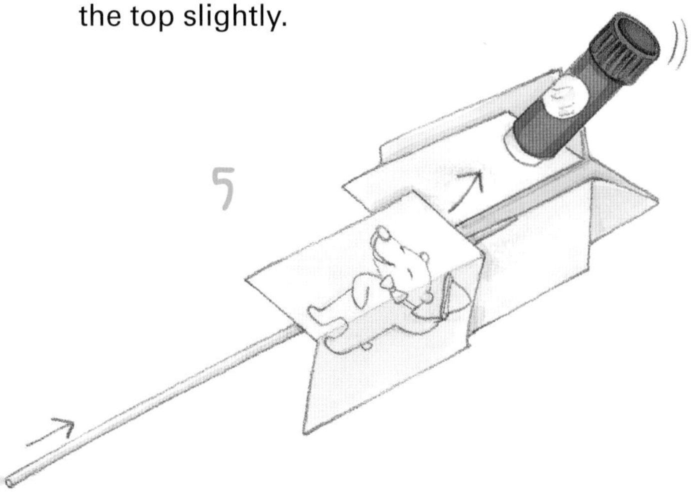

Why does it happen?

When you spin your home movie theater, you do the same thing as when you watch a cartoon film. In fact, you are seeing one drawing after the other, but these drawings go by very fast and your eyes see them as continuous movement. This is called **persistence of vision**. It sounds strange but means that your brain retains all the images you see for just a moment and quickly combines them with the next image, instead of seeing them one by one.

6 Try it out!

Now you have your own movie theater! There are only 4 scenes, but they're wonderful, aren't they? To see the figure in movement, you must spin the skewer very fast. ENJOY THE MOVIE!

Magical Experiments with Light & Color

First edition for the United States and Canada published in 2014 by Barron's Educational Series, Inc.

Copyright © Gemser Publications, S.L. 2014
C/ Castell, 38; Teià (08329) Barcelona, Spain (World Rights)
Tel: 93 540 13 53
E-mail: info@mercedesros.com
Website: mercedesros.com

Text: Paula Navarro & Àngels Jiménez

Illustrations: Bernadette Cuxart

Design and layout: Estudi Guasch, S.L.

All inquiries should be addressed to:
Barron's Educational Series, Inc.
250 Wireless Boulevard
Hauppauge, New York 11788
www.barronseduc.com

ISBN: 978-1-4380-0426-6

Library of Congress Control
  Number: 2013943428

Date of Manufacture: May 2014
Place of Manufacture: L. REX PRINTING
  COMPANY LIMITED, Dongguan City,
  Guangdong, China

Printed in China
9 8 7 6 5 4 3 2 1